The

ROMAN WRITING TABLETS

from Vindolanda

THE ROMAN WRITING TABLETS FROM VINDOLANDA

ALAN K. BOWMAN

BMP

Published for the Trustees of the British Museum
by British Museum Publications Ltd

The cover shows a tablet containing a complete letter written by Niger and Brocchus, possibly from Ribchester, to Flavius Cerialis, commander of the Eighth Cohort of Batavians at Vindolanda.

Published by British Museum Publications Ltd,
46 Bloomsbury Street, London WC1B 3QQ

British Library Cataloguing in Publication Data

Bowman, Alan K.
Roman writing tablets from Vindolanda.
1. Tablets (Paleography 2. Chesterholm (Northumberland)—Antiquities
I. Title
936.2'8'81 DA147.V56

ISBN 0-7141-1373-5

Designed by Norman Ball
Drawings by Philip Compton

Set in Linotron Ehrhardt by
Rowland Phototypesetting Ltd
and printed in Great Britain by
St Edmundsbury Press
Bury St Edmunds, Suffolk

CONTENTS

AUTHOR'S ACKNOWLEDGEMENTS

I should like to make it clear that everything in this book is based upon a programme of research carried out jointly with my co-author of the *Britannia* monograph, Dr J. D. Thomas of the University of Durham. Whilst he can carry no responsibility for what I have said here, my debt to him is immense. Equally, many scholars and institutions have played their part in the framing of the conclusions that are advanced here: full acknowledgement is made in the monograph, but I should like to make special mention here of the support provided by IBM (UK) Ltd; Rank Xerox (UK) Ltd; Kodak Ltd; and BP (Chemicals Division). Finally, I should like to record my gratitude to the Trustees of the British Museum for inviting me to write this general account of this major find; and to the Department of Prehistoric and Romano-British Antiquities and to British Museum Publications Ltd for their help and co-operation.

A. K. BOWMAN

PHOTOGRAPHIC ACKNOWLEDGEMENTS

The author and publishers are grateful to the following for permission to reproduce photographs: The Ashmolean Museum, Oxford (fig. 12), R. E. Birley (figs 2, 3), The British Library (fig. 5), Editions d'Art Albert Skira (fig. 7), The Egypt Exploration Society (fig. 14), Grosvenor Museum, Chester (fig. 1), The Museum of Antiquities of the University and Society of Antiquaries of Newcastle upon Tyne (fig. 16), University of Cambridge Committee for Aerial Photography (fig. 4), University of Newcastle upon Tyne (figs 8, 20, 24), The Vindolanda Trust (fig. 6).

INTRODUCTION

In the spring of 1973, excavations directed by Mr Robin Birley at the Roman fort of Vindolanda (modern Chesterholm), close to Hadrian's Wall, brought to light the first of a remarkable series of more than two hundred wooden writing tablets. As the oldest group of written documents known from Britain, they comprise a discovery of first-rate historical importance. It seems that the tablets were deposited between about AD 95 and 105—a decade or two before work began on the construction of Hadrian's Wall—and consist mainly of letters, accounts and other material relating to the administration of the fort. As such, they provide us with an extraordinary insight into the life of the times, seen both from the point of view of senior officers and from that of more humble soldiers. Here are stock-checks on supplies; personal letters of recommendation; the record of a gift of fifty oysters; and even the description of a parcel from home containing socks, sandals and two pairs of underpants! When taken in conjunction with references to people and to places, they are a source of information hitherto unparalleled in the northern provinces of the Roman Empire, and thus form a major addition to the National collections of the British Museum.

Most of the tablets consist of thin leaves of wood, a type hardly recognised until now, but one probably in very common use in antiquity. The texts are generally written in ink, and it says much for the skill of Dr Bowman and his colleague, Dr J. D. Thomas, that they have been able to interpret the handwriting of these long-forgotten scribes. Their definitive catalogue, *Vindolanda: The Latin Writing Tablets* is published as *Britannia* Monograph no. 4 (1983), but in this book Dr Bowman has provided us with a concise account for the general reader, prepared especially for those who have seen the tablets on display in the Romano-British gallery and who want to know more about this wonderful find and its implications.

Naturally, we are able to display only a very small number of the tablets in the gallery. These have been carefully selected by Dr Bowman to illustrate the wide range of information that the tablets contain; several of the texts are reproduced, together with a full commentary, in this book. Meanwhile, we have the task of safeguarding this unique collection of highly delicate objects, a responsibility best met by rigorous control of the humidity levels both in the gallery case and in the reserve archive; and by as little handling of the tablets as possible. When one reflects how all too rarely archaeological evidence provides such personal glimpses into the past, then it will be obvious how carefully one must monitor the condition of these rare and precious pages of history. We can therefore be grateful to Dr Bowman for providing us with this absorbing account of the tablets. However unspectacular they may appear in comparison with, say, the Mildenhall or Thetford Treasure, their appeal is universal: for, above all, they are about people and not things, and conjure up an intimate picture of life on this isolated military outpost some nineteen hundred years ago.

T. W. POTTER
Assistant Keeper
British Museum

1 *Tombstone of an* optio *(a centurion's deputy) called Caecilius Avitus. He was an officer in the Twentieth Legion, based at Chester, and is here shown with staff in his right hand and a case for writing tablets in his left. Many of his duties were clerical.*

THE TABLETS AND THEIR BACKGROUND

Vindolanda and the Roman frontier

By the beginning of the second century of our era, the Romans had come into possession of a vast empire which stretched from Newcastle-upon-Tyne in north Britain to the Euphrates river in Syria. This enormous area naturally embraced a wide variety of peoples and customs, of social and religious institutions, of artistic and building styles. In short, it was probably not much more homogeneous as a 'culture' or 'civilisation' than it is today.

There was, however, one force whose presence was felt in all the areas of that empire at one time or another—the Roman army. This was much more than a well-organised and highly efficient fighting machine, though it certainly was that. It was the main instrument through which Rome achieved the pacification of her provinces, often enough by direct force in the first instance, but then through a process of encouraging urbanisation and settlement, higher agricultural productivity, more extensive networks of trade and commerce which usually followed routes primarily established for military reasons, and the development of appropriate social and religious institutions.

By AD 100 these processes were well advanced in some places, like Spain and Gaul, which had been under Roman rule for more than two centuries—so much so that by this time there were many Gauls and Spaniards who had taken their place among the ruling aristocracy of the Empire as Roman senators. But Britain was a relative newcomer to the Empire, having been made into a province by the Emperor Claudius in AD 43, and the initial conquest

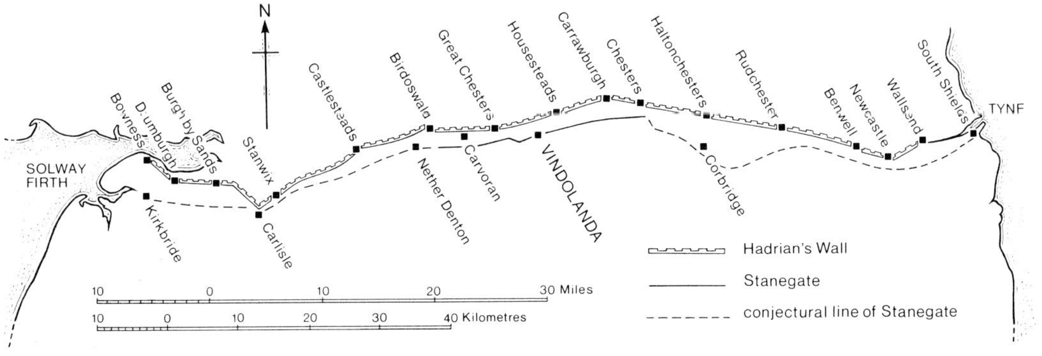

2 Plan of the Stanegate frontier and of Hadrian's Wall, which replaced it as the main frontier line in the 120s AD.

brought direct Roman rule at first only to the south-eastern part of Britain, the territory bounded by the Fosse Way, running from Lincoln to Exeter. The gradual extension of Roman rule into northern Britain took place in the last three decades of the first century AD and it is at the end of this period that we find the northern frontier being established on the so-called Stanegate Line (fig. 2). This was a road and ditch system connecting the main frontier forts, Stanwix, Nether Denton, Chesterholm (Vindolanda) and Corbridge, and it retained its importance until the building of Hadrian's Wall, a few miles further to the north (*c.* AD 122–5).

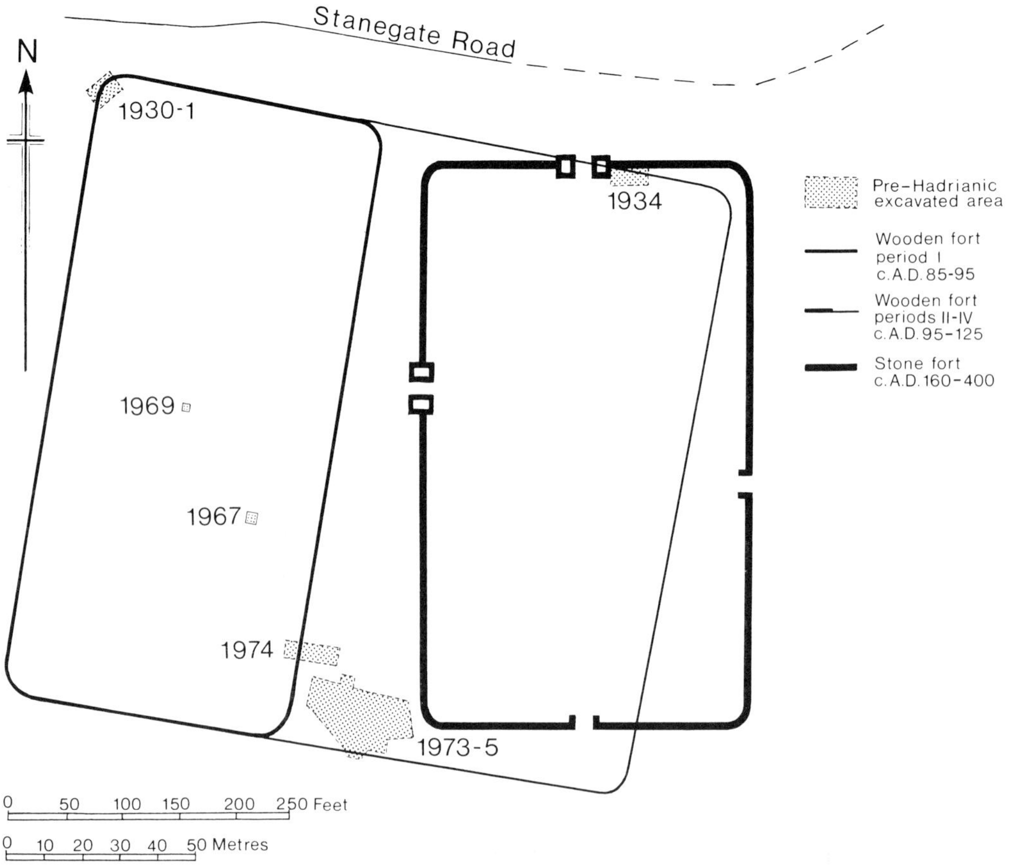

3 Plan of the pre-Hadrianic timber forts and the later stone fort at Vindolanda. The later fort is on the right. The earlier fort was probably built in two phases, the first consisting of the left-hand part of the area and the second a rebuilding which adapted and enlarged the original plan.

Thus the pre-Hadrianic timber forts at Vindolanda (fig. 3), dating to the period *c.* AD 85–125, before the Wall was constructed a few years after the beginning of Hadrian's reign in 117, make an important contribution to our knowledge of the Roman frontier in Britain at this time. It would be erroneous to think of this frontier as a strict line of demarcation between Roman and non-Roman territory. Although the development of the Stanegate Line as a frontier was taking place during the two decades following the governorship of Agricola (AD 78–84), it is certain that the Romans maintained a presence in southern Scotland during this period, only completing the withdrawal to the Stanegate Line during the first few years of the second century. This line, which linked a series of strategically placed military posts, must thus be seen both as a guarantee of the protection of those areas of northern England most recently taken under direct Roman rule and as a basis for the exertion of a degree of military and diplomatic control over areas further to the north which were not under direct Roman rule. The aim of such a policy was to create conditions favourable to further annexation of territory, but the withdrawal from southern Scotland and the building of Hadrian's Wall probably indicate that the Romans recognised the impracticability of further expansion at this time.

4 The later stone fort at Vindolanda, built in the third century. The pre-Hadrianic excavation area, in which the writing tablets were found, is at the south-west corner of this fort.

The Roman army has left an indelible mark on the province of Britain, particularly in the north of England. Military building techniques had an important influence on the development of civilian settlements. The extensive road networks owe their origins to the military engineers and focus, of course, on the great legionary fortresses of York, Chester and Caerleon. These fortresses, however, were well within the pacified territory and the road and frontier systems, as a consequence, depended to a large extent for their efficiency and protection on the additional presence of a large number of auxiliary units (five-hundred- or a thousand-strong infantry cohorts and *alae* of a thousand cavalrymen) stationed both on and behind the frontier lines. Vindolanda was garrisoned by auxiliary cohorts during the period when it formed part of the Stanegate frontier. After the building of Hadrian's Wall part of its former strategic role was taken over by the fort at Housesteads, on the Wall itself. But Vindolanda's continuing military importance is clearly shown by the existence of two stone forts, the first of which was perhaps built in the later part of the second century, the second in the later part of the third century (fig. 4).

Documentation of the Roman army

In the first two centuries AD Britain, Germany and the Danube provinces were the areas of the Roman Empire in which the military presence of Rome was most clearly felt. Any reconstruction of the story of Roman pacification of these areas has to rely heavily on the evidence of archaeology and inscriptions on stone, for the ancient literary sources naturally paid relatively little attention to the detailed history of the development of these provinces. The archaeological and inscriptional evidence is a very necessary supplement since it enables us to identify the locations of forts, to perceive changes in size or structure and to estimate their role in the defensive system as a whole.

There is quite a lot of evidence of this sort for Vindolanda in the period before the building of Hadrian's Wall. It enables us to see that it began to develop as a frontier station in the mid-80s AD as a timber-built fort covering about three and a half acres; some ten years later it was enlarged to an area of about eight acres, probably reflecting a greater firmness in the frontier system. The archaeological evidence for the timber structures of the forts, the variety of artefacts found (particularly organic remains and leather goods), combine to make this site one of the most important in Britain for our knowledge of the history of the province between AD 85 and 125.

But this is inevitably only part of the story. Vegetius, a Roman writer of the fourth century AD, who wrote a treatise on military affairs, emphatically noted the intricate bureaucracy of the Roman army and stressed the enormous amount of documentation which such a bureaucracy generated. Since the organisation of the army was fairly uniform, this must obviously have applied to the army in Britain as much as anywhere else. Yet, until the discovery of the writing tablets in Vindolanda, not a scrap of this documentation had survived from Britain. Our knowledge of the organisation of the army was derived from surviving documents from other parts of the Roman Empire where the physical conditions were

5 *British Library Papyrus no. 2851. This papyrus, from about* AD *100–105, was discovered in Egypt and records the assignments of soldiers belonging to a military unit serving in the province of Lower Moesia.*

conducive to the preservation of papyrus, the material upon which such records were normally written in these areas.

Thus almost all our information of this kind comes from two places: Egypt, which has yielded documents from a variety of different sites covering the period of the first three centuries AD, and Dura-Europos, a frontier post on the Euphrates in Syria, whose importance lasted roughly from the middle of the second century AD to the middle of the third. Amongst the invaluable finds at this site was part of the documentary archive of its unit, the Twentieth Cohort of Palmyrene Archers. Although this material comes from areas in which the main language used and spoken was Greek, the military documents are in Latin, which was the official language of the Roman army. It is worth stressing, however, that such Latin military documents form a very small proportion indeed of the total number of papyri which have survived from Egypt. The vast majority are in Greek and relate either to the civil administration of the province or to the private affairs of Greek-speaking individuals.

The value of the military documents from Egypt and Dura-Europos is immense, for they give us a great deal of detailed information concerning the internal organisation of the army and its relationship with the populace and institutions of the province in which the particular units were stationed. Pay records of legionary soldiers in Egypt show, for instance, that the standard rate of pay for ordinary soldiers (225 denarii per year until the beginning of the reign of the Emperor Domitian, AD 81–96) was subject to deductions at source for food, clothing and other items. The highly ordered routine of the military camp can also be observed in surviving duty rosters which specify the tasks to which individual soldiers or groups of soldiers were detailed. Personnel records allow us to estimate the strength of particular units and illustrate patterns of recruitment and discharge. There is some evidence for the organisation of the commissariat and for the religious festivals observed as an official feature of Roman military life. A few documents show us that soldiers were often detached for duties away from their home base. Occasionally something surprising turns up, as for instance a papyrus found in Egypt which records details of detached service in a unit which was serving in the Danubian province of Moesia in about AD 100 (fig. 5).

Apart from this, there is a considerable amount of information which is less official and more peripheral but nevertheless casts an important light on the role of the army as an institution of great social and economic importance in the provinces. There is evidence for the status of soldiers and veterans, for the legal and economic privileges which service in the army conferred and for the rules applying to marriage, the status of children and the right to bequeath property. And this information is most valuably supplemented by papyri which give us the 'soldier's-eye view' of life in and around the Roman army. Soldiers maintained contact with their families and friends and wrote letters, often in Latin which their military service forced them to learn if it was not their native tongue, in which they described or referred to the more mundane aspects of life under the Roman standard.

Given the amount and variety of information supplied by the papyri, it would be unrealistic to expect that the writing tablets from Vindolanda would enlarge our knowledge of the Roman army by supplying us with new kinds of documents. In fact, the information in them lies within the range just described. What is particularly valuable is the fact that they yield evidence of this kind for an area in which it was previously completely lacking.

The discovery of the writing tablets

The sensational discovery of the Vindolanda writing tablets in the spring of 1973 cannot be better described than by the account of Robin Birley, the archaeologist who found them. 'If I have to spend the rest of my life working in dirty, wet trenches, I doubt whether I shall ever again experience the shock and excitement I felt at my first glimpse of ink hieroglyphics on tiny scraps of wood . . . I came across two small, thin fragments of wood which looked rather like oily plane shavings. I wondered if this was evidence for wood-working on the spot and passed the fragment up to my assistant on the surface for his opinion. He examined the wood and passed it back to me, observing that it seemed to have some peculiar marks on it. I had another look and thought I must have been dreaming, for the marks appeared to be ink writing. We took the piece over to the excavation hut and gently cleaned it, discovering that there were in fact two slivers of wood adhering to each other. After gently prising them apart with a knife, we stared at the tiny writing in utter disbelief.' This tablet proved to contain a letter about clothing (no. 5, see pp. 45–6).

Once the nature of this object had been realised, the archaeologists conducted a painstaking search for more examples in 1974 and 1975 and the fruits of their labour were a total of over two hundred tablets or groups of fragments, of which somewhat over half contained some writing. The process of excavation itself presented considerable difficulties because the wooden fragments were so fragile that the danger of breakage was very high. Furthermore, they were embedded in layers of ancient flooring which could not be easily dissected in the trench. The best solution to these difficulties was to cut out the flooring in sections, like peat, and transport it to the surface where it could be more easily dissected, layer by layer.

A second, more immediate problem arose from the alarming fact that the writing on the first tablet discovered began to fade rapidly when it was exposed to the air. In fact, this proved to be less serious than was at first feared because writing in carbon-based ink, which was the only kind in common use at this period, can be recovered relatively easily by the techniques of infra-red photography even when it is invisible to the naked eye. But this did raise the related issue of conservation of the tablets—since such material had never been discovered before there was no standard technique for conserving it. It was an important advance in scientific archaeology, therefore, that experts at the British Museum's Research Laboratory were soon able to develop such a technique, which involved prolonged soaking of the tablets in alternate baths of methyl alcohol and ether. Treated thus, the tablets dried out with very little shrinkage and the writing was preserved and clearly visible in those cases where it had not already faded.

One important feature of the discovery was that there was sufficient information in the archaeological context to indicate the general nature of the deposit of writing tablets. Much of the area covered by the pre-Hadrianic forts at Vindolanda is overlaid by the second- and third-century stone forts and the civilian settlement (*vicus*) to the west of it. But it was possible to excavate a small area in the south of the pre-Hadrianic part, at the south-west corner of the second/third-century fort. The pre-Hadrianic forts dated to the period roughly between AD 85 and 125 and show a sequence of a smaller timber fort followed by a larger one, perhaps built some time in the 90s (fig. 3). The tablet deposit was in the centre of the southern boundary of this larger fort and could therefore be dated to the period beginning *c.* AD 95.

The tablets were found in compacted layers of bracken and straw flooring which also contained a great quantity and variety of remains, both organic and inorganic. The dates assigned to the successive layers of flooring suggested that the great majority of the tablets came from the period AD 95–110, although there are a few in the higher and later layers. This was strikingly confirmed by a tablet which clearly referred to a man who was known to have been governor of Britain in AD 103 (no. 4, see pp. 41–4).

The organic remains in this flooring included gorse-pods, heather and twigs but there was also the residue of human occupation in the shape of bones, oyster-shells, leather, jewellery, cloth and wooden implements, as well as a considerable quantity of human excrement and urine. The nature and variety of these remains suggest that this was probably a rubbish dump of some sort and the presence of the writing tablets may be explained by the fact that they were thrown out when they became out of date. It is noteworthy that the edges of some of the tablets show signs of having been burnt. The nearest building to this dump seems to have been a factory or workshop (*fabrica*) and it is probable that this dump is connected with it. The large amount of urine in the area may be due to the fact that it was used in the process of tanning which was carried out in the workshop (fig. 6). Again, an interesting light is cast on this by one of the military documents in the collection which records the assignment of 343 men to the *fabricae*.

6 Footwear found in the pre-Hadrianic area at Vindolanda. It is probable that there was a tannery close to this part of the fort.

At first, the survival of the tablets in such a good state of preservation was thought to be largely due to the extraordinary chemical conditions in this area. Clay compactions between the layers of flooring created pockets of anaerobic (oxygen-free) conditions and tannin, produced by the organic remains and assisted by the presence of leather, enhanced the preservative factors. It is interesting that an earlier find of writing tablets, of which very few contain any legible writing, however, turned up in very similar conditions at the fortress of Vindonissa in Switzerland. However, it is true that some tablets were preserved in the later layers at Vindolanda where the conditions are markedly different. So it may well be that the failure to discover similar written material on a significant scale at other sites is due not so much to the fact that tablets have not survived in the ground as to the fact that they have simply not been recognised for what they are. And, in fact, since the Vindolanda discoveries, sporadic finds at Ribchester, Lechlade and Carlisle (though not remotely comparable to Vindolanda in number or in the quantity and quality of writing preserved) now suggest that in future such material might be more common.

As far as Vindolanda itself is concerned, there is a high degree of probability that there are many more tablets awaiting discovery in the ground. But their recovery requires prolonged excavation at deep levels and careful conservation of all the different kinds of material found at these levels. These processes are very expensive indeed and cannot be resumed on a significant scale until more financial resources can be found.

7 A wall-painting from Pompeii showing a girl holding a set of wooden writing tablets and a metal stylus.

The nature of the tablets

One of the most important features of the Vindolanda writing tablets is that they make a significant contribution to our knowledge of writing and writing materials in the Roman world. This is because the great majority of the tablets—all but a dozen or so—are of a kind almost totally unknown before this discovery. Stylus tablets, that is, thickish slabs of wood, hollowed out in the centre and filled with wax which was designed to take writing incised with the tip of a metal stylus, are very well known and were generally assumed to be the commonest medium for writing in wood (figs 7–9). But most of the Vindolanda tablets are quite different: they are thin slices of wood which were evidently designed for writing in ink. And their great preponderance in this collection over the dozen or so stylus tablets suggests that they might have been very much more common in the Roman world generally.

There are, in fact, a few pieces of evidence in classical literature for the existence of such tablets. The clearest description is given by the historian Herodian, a Greek writer who lived about the middle of the third century AD. In one passage he refers to tablets 'of the kind made out of lime-wood cut into thin slivers and folded face to face by being bent'. As we shall see, this amounts to a very accurate description of the type of tablets found at Vindolanda, except for one detail. The Vindolanda examples are not made from lime-wood but from birch or alder. This inconsistency is not so very surprising since Herodian is likely to have been familiar with practices in the more southerly parts of the Mediterranean world where the lime was common. But the lime is not native to the Vindolanda region and, since such tablets were evidently cheap and easy to make for local use, one would expect to find the native woods utilised.

The dimensions of the leaves are of the order of 16 to 20 cm × 6 to 9 cm (the larger dimension being that parallel to the grain of the wood). In the majority of cases the thickness of the leaf is between 1 and 2 mm, sometimes as much as 3 mm; but more striking, in a significant number of cases, is the extreme thinness—less than 0.25 mm. Normally the surface is very fine-grained and smooth and had been prepared expressly for writing in ink.

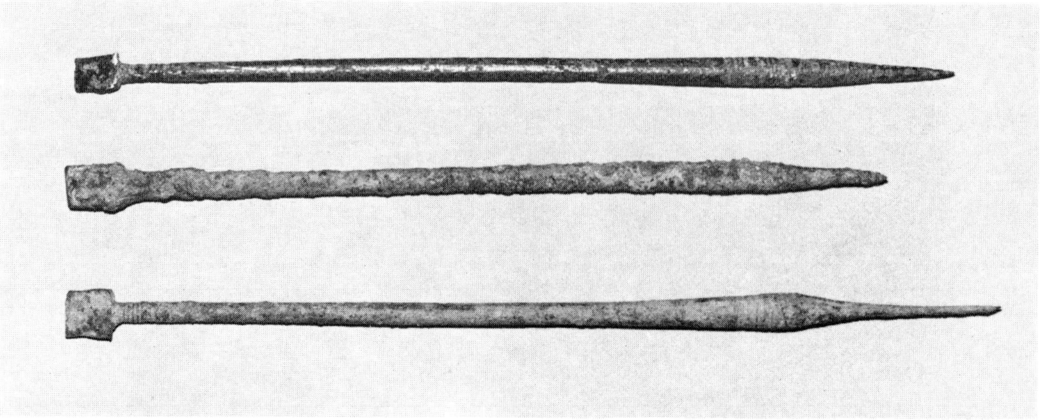

8 Metal styli from Vindolanda. These pens were used for writing on wax-filled wooden tablets of the kind shown in fig. 9.

The tablets would have been extremely supple when first cut and capable of being folded across the grain without breaking. Technical analysis has shown that they were cut from the sapwood of very young trees, possibly with the use of a spokeshave or a very sharp knife with a long blade. In view of the high degree of expertise which Roman craftsmen attained in cutting veneers for decorating furniture, it is easy to imagine that the technique of making such tablets will have been well known.

The leaves thus manufactured were used in different ways, depending on the nature of the text written on them. Most of the letters (which, it should be remembered, must have come from a variety of places in Britain, and perhaps also Gaul) are identical in format (fig. 10). The writer used the broad edges of the leaf as top and bottom and wrote his letter in two columns (of which the right-hand one is generally broader than the left). He then scored the leaf vertically down the centre, folded the right-hand section over to meet the left and wrote the address on the back of the right-hand half. Several leaves have matched notches cut in both the left- and right-hand edges and these were probably used as anchors for binding strings which were tied round the letters, no doubt in order to preserve the written text and to keep it from the eyes of inquisitive letter-carriers.

Some of the official documents were also written in this way, parallel with the grain of the wood, but unfortunately none of these gives us more than half of a full-sized leaf, so it is impossible to be sure that the double column format will have been used.

9 *One of about a dozen stylus tablets discovered in the writing-tablet deposit at Vindolanda. Traces of writing can be seen where the metal stylus has penetrated the original wax covering and left scratches on the wood beneath.*

Much more striking is the way in which the leaves were used for accounts. Here the writer would use the narrow dimension of the leaf as top and bottom, with the grain running vertically, and would write his accounts in narrow columns. The most remarkable example of this is the account of food supplies (no. 1) which consists of a series of such leaves, with tie-holes and notches in the top and bottom edges of each leaf. Here the writer has scored the leaves across the centre horizontally, but instead of tying the top edge of each leaf to its own bottom edge he has tied it to the bottom edge of the preceding leaf. The result is a sort of wooden notebook in a concertina format, which is unique (figs 11, 18 and 19). Anyone who wanted to read this account would simply grasp the top and bottom pieces of the bundle and pull them apart in a vertical motion.

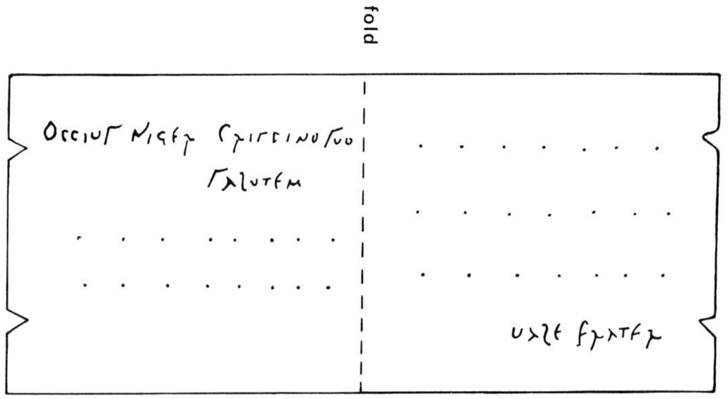

10 Drawing illustrating the manner in which wooden leaves were used for letters. The text was written on the inner face in two columns; the leaf was then folded and the address was written on the back of the right-hand section. The notches in the left and right-hand edges were probably intended as anchors for binding cords which were tied round the outside of the letter.

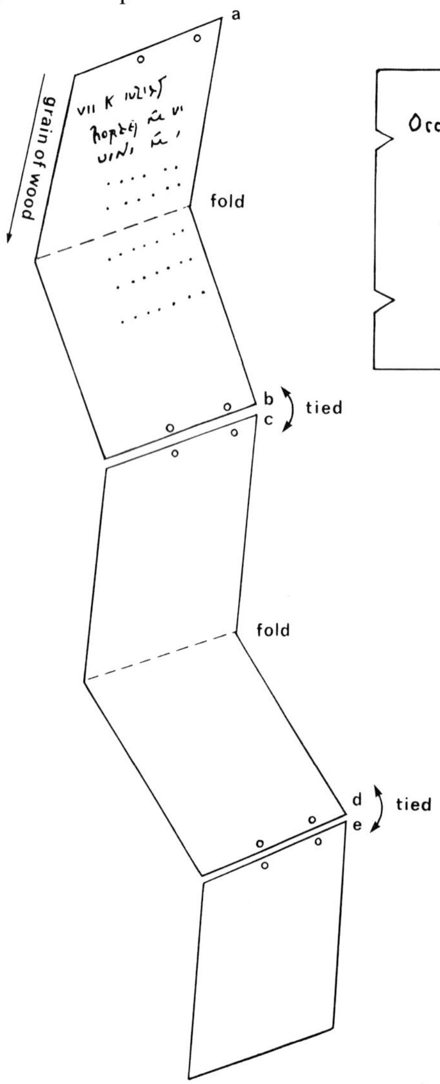

11 Drawing illustrating the concertina format used for the accounts of food supplies (nos 1 and 2). The holes bored in the top and bottom edges of the leaves were made for thongs which tied the leaves together.

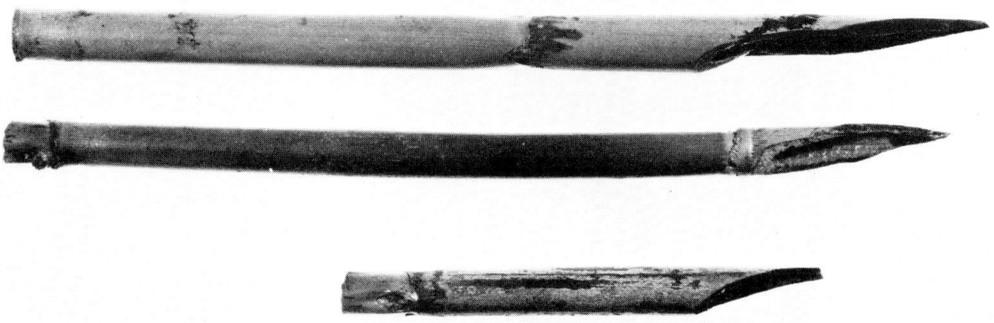

12 Reed pens discovered in Egypt. These pens were used for writing in ink on papyrus and wooden tablets of the leaf type in the Vindolanda collection.

As writing material, these leaves bear a strong resemblance to papyri, many thousands of which have been found in Egypt. Like the papyri, they are written with a reed pen (fig. 12) and an ink manufactured from carbon, gum arabic and water (the use of iron-gall ink was not introduced until much later). They are also remarkably similar to the papyri in the kind of scripts they show and in the conventions they employ; this is especially notable since the tablets come from the opposite extreme of the Roman Empire. It is important to emphasise, however, that most of the papyri from Egypt are written in Greek, with only a very small percentage in Latin. The Vindolanda tablets therefore offer us a unique opportunity to study, through a large number of examples written in different hands, the way in which Latin cursive or 'business' script was written in the late first and early second centuries. Indeed, from this point of view it would be fair to describe the Vindolanda writing tablets as the most important material yet discovered.

The scripts all fall broadly into the category which experts in palaeography have called 'Old Roman Cursive', a type of writing current in the first two centuries of our era. By 'cursive' they mean a business type of script, with small, unelaborate characters, which was used for documents and letters, as opposed to 'literary bookhands' which used capital forms of the letters. These Latin cursive hands are extremely difficult to read, not only because the Vindolanda tablets frequently contain only part of a text with words, letters or whole lines abraded or missing, but also because many of the individual letter forms are almost impossible to differentiate one from another unless there is enough of the text surviving to provide a basis for analysis of the letter forms used by that particular writer. Thus, for instance, in some texts the letters *c*, *p*, *a*, *t* and *s* can be very difficult to distinguish and progress in reading the words can often be made only by a tedious process of trying various possibilities until some sense emerges. This is especially true of private letters in which, unlike some official documents, it is impossible to predict the content on the basis of parallels with other examples.

There are various other conventions and practices which emerge as a pattern only after long study and comparison of the different tablets. Writers of Latin cursive at this time used virtually no punctuation. Sometimes they separated words by a dot written on a level with the middle of their letters, but even writers who normally used this did not do so consistently. Many writers used no dots and did not even leave spaces between words, and those who did, again, did so inconsistently. Fairly frequently words were abbreviated, sometimes with a mark indicating abbreviation, sometimes without. All this makes these texts a far different proposition from the elegant bookhands which are found in medieval manuscripts or ancient papyri containing literary works (fig. 14).

What is interesting, however, is the fact that patterns *do* emerge. In spite of the variety of different hands, the letter forms are, broadly speaking, within the same family and we can add one or two oddities which do not fit into patterns established on the basis of previously known material, and thus modify the pattern. The writers of private letters invariably use the same double column format, putting their own name and the name of the addressee in the first line and the word *salutem* ('greetings') in the second line, usually at the right. If the letter has been written by a clerk, the author often adds a final line of greeting in his own hand. The addresses written on the backs of the letters employ a slightly different kind of script, not a capital script but a cursive type in which the letters are larger and more elongated. But one must be prepared for the occasional surprise. A fragment of a tablet containing what must have been part of a letter presents us with an elegant example of calligraphic handwriting in which the writer's use of thick and thin strokes of the pen is much more appropriate to what is normally characterised as the literary bookhand than the ordinary cursive (fig. 15).

13 Inkpot and a bronze pen, found in London, dating to the second century AD. *The inkpot is inscribed with the owner's name.*

14 Papyrus from Quaṣr Ibrîm (Egyptian Nubia), probably dating to the late first century BC, *which contains elegiacs by the Roman poet Cornelius Gallus. One of the earliest examples of this type of Latin bookhand.*

15 A fragment of a tablet from Vindolanda written in a very elegant hand. The alternating use of thick and thin strokes is particularly noteworthy. Scale 2:1.

What the tablets tell us

The examples presented below are representative of the material in the whole collection but they contain only part of the information which can be derived from it. There are several important respects in which the collection as a whole makes a really significant contribution to our knowledge.

First, it must be said that the Vindolanda writing tablets are of just as much value for what they are as for what the texts on them actually tell us directly. Two particular aspects need to be emphasised.

Most of the tablets themselves are of a very unusual type, being made of thin slices or leaves of wood made to take writing in ink. Until the discovery of the Vindolanda tablets, it was normally believed that tablets of the stylus type were the commonest medium for writing in wood. But the Vindolanda collection indicates that in reality wooden leaves made for ink writing may have been much more common for ephemeral documents of all kinds in those areas of the Empire where papyrus was difficult and expensive to obtain. That they have not been discovered until very recently may be due to various factors: stylus tablets are much more likely to turn up in isolated finds because they are sturdier and more durable and because they tended to contain documents of a legal nature which might be more carefully preserved in antiquity; the leaf tablets are so difficult to recognise in the archaeological context that it is possible that their existence at many sites has in fact been overlooked. Archaeologists therefore owe a debt of gratitude to Vindolanda in that they are now aware of the possibility of the existence of such documentation.

A second area of particular value is the light these tablets cast upon the history and development of Latin handwriting. Until the Vindolanda discovery, our knowledge of Latin palaeography was based largely upon the material from Egypt and from Dura-Europos. The papyri from Dura are almost all from the first half of the third century AD and Egyptian papyri in Latin from the first and second centuries are fairly few and far between; nor do they form a unified body of material either in date or provenance. What is truly remarkable about the Vindolanda tablets, therefore, is the fact that they contain a great variety of different hands (about eighty in all), which can be assigned with confidence to a period not longer than about twenty or thirty years. All must originate in the north-western provinces of the Empire (the military documents, of course, must have been written at Vindolanda itself; most of the letters come from elsewhere, but probably not from very far afield). It is this feature which makes the Vindolanda writing tablets an immensely important contribution to the study of early Latin handwriting.

The tablets show two things in particular: first, that despite the great variety of hands, the scripts are in general closely comparable to those found on Egyptian papyri from this period. This makes it possible to assert with some confidence that Latin cursive was written in much the same way at this period in all parts of the Empire. Second, detailed study of the individual letter forms has given us a clearer picture of the relationship between the type of script in use in the first and second centuries and the very different type of script which developed from the beginning of the third century.

Documents and letters of this kind rarely tell us anything about events of great political importance but it would be wrong to suppose that the Vindolanda tablets do not contain information of great value; especially since the period from which they come (*c.* AD 95–105) is very poorly represented by evidence of any kind.

The official military documents have a particular value, of course. Some record the activities of the soldiers at Vindolanda. In one document, a total number of 343 men is detailed to the workshops (*fabricae*) and the more specific assignments of these men in groups suggest that most of them were engaged in construction work, collecting materials, building a bath-house and a hospital, plastering and working at the kilns. Since this text might well date to the period when the fort was enlarged from three and a half to eight acres, it is tempting to connect this building activity with the increase in size and facilities. Another document perhaps refers to the manufacture of shields and swords in the workshops at Vindolanda. Such information serves to remind us that activities of this kind were by no means confined to the legionary units of the Roman army.

The military accounts of which nos 1 and 2 are the best examples are now the most informative documents of this type that we possess. They show the system of accounting for receipts or disbursements of food on a daily basis and illustrate the range of commodities in use in a Roman fort: barley, Celtic beer, vintage wine, sour wine, fish-sauce, lard, salt, spices, wheat and a variety of meats, ham, pork, roe-deer and venison. The latter, in particular, give good reason to be sceptical of the view that meat was eaten only rarely in the Roman army.

The tablets give us valuable information concerning the identity of the units which occupied Vindolanda in this period. Here, paradoxically, the letters are of more use than the official documents for it is in their addresses that we find mention of the name of the units. There seem to have been two auxiliary cohorts at Vindolanda. One was the Eighth Cohort of Batavians, which was previously unknown. It is probable that this was a five-hundred-strong

16 Sextarius-measure from Carvoran. The sextarius is used as a measure for dry goods and liquids in the account of food supplies (no 1). Scale 2:1.

cohort, part-mounted (*cohors quingenaria equitata*) (see fig. 17). The other is the First Tungrian Cohort, a one-thousand-strong infantry unit, which was already known from other sources; by the third century it was in garrison at Housesteads but whether it moved there directly from Vindolanda after the building of Hadrian's Wall is uncertain. It seems likely that both these units occupied Vindolanda during the period AD 95–105, and the most probable sequence of occupation is that the larger Tungrian cohort succeeded the Batavian unit after the enlargement of the fort (in which the Batavian unit was perhaps involved). Both of these units will have been raised in an area which is now in Belgium or the Netherlands and it is interesting to note that Tacitus mentions Batavian and Tungrian units in action under Agricola at the famous battle of Mons Graupius which took place in AD 84 somewhere in the north of Scotland.

The tablets contain little evidence apart from this for military dispositions, but there is one very important mention of the existence of a centurion in charge of a region (*centurio regionarius*) based at Carlisle (no. 3). Finally, there is good reason to believe that two of the letters sent to Vindolanda came from the commander of the Roman fort of Bremetennacum (Ribchester), an important military post on the route between Chester and the northern frontier. One of the letters refers to the fact that soldiers of the Tungrian cohort had passed through on their way to deliver letters to the governor of the province, who was perhaps at Chester.

More usually, however, the letters are of a more mundane kind. Of great interest is the fact that it has been possible to identify three small archives, groups of letters addressed to individuals. The first is the archive of Flavius Cerialis, who was the commander of the Eighth Batavian Cohort, the second that of a man named Crispinus who was in command of the First Tungrian Cohort and the third belongs to a man named Flavius Genialis, who was certainly also an officer. The archive of Cerialis is the most informative and contains, apart from a very interesting letter of recommendation (no. 3, pp. 37–40), a note from Ribchester which tantalisingly refers to the fact that Cerialis is soon to meet the governor of the province. Crispinus was the recipient of the other letter from Ribchester, mentioned above.

There are many other letters which cannot be assigned to any of these archives. The most important of these is certainly the draft letter, written at Vindolanda, which contains a reference to the governor of Britain, Lucius Neratius Marcellus (no. 4). This rather elegant epistle certainly emanates from the officer class of the army. So perhaps also does the fragment of a letter in which the writer refers to a gift of fifty oysters sent to him by a friend from a place called Cordonovi, which cannot be identified with any known Roman place-name (no. 6). But the letter detailing the despatch of various items of clothing—socks, sandals and underpants—is more likely to concern people of a rather more humble rank (no. 5).

In some ways the private letters evoke the life and milieu of the Roman officer or soldier more vividly than the official documents, but often enough they are obscure and difficult to explain precisely because they *are* private letters to and from individuals who will have known what they were referring to much better than we can. Only rarely do we catch a glimpse of the great Roman Empire outside the province of Britain: there is one fragment of a letter in which the writer seems to be referring to an impending trip to Rome and it is fascinating—although not perhaps so very surprising—to find the name of the metropolis turning up at the furthest boundary of the Empire.

17 An auxiliary cavalryman in action, as shown on Trajan's Column in Rome. The Column was dedicated in AD *113, close to the period when the tablets were deposited.*

A SELECTION OF TEXTS

Notes on conventions employed in the texts

Square brackets indicate that a number of letters or words are missing. Where letters are printed inside square brackets they are restored either because the sense of the text demands it or from parallels in other documents.

The use of round brackets indicates the expansion of an abbreviation in the original text. Thus *m(odii)* represents the original $\overline{m}$. Sometimes abbreviations are not marked at all on the tablet, e.g. *praef* for *praef(ecto)*. Sometimes the writer may use a symbol, e.g. 𐆖 (*denarii*) or *f* (*sextarii*).

<> indicates letters missing in the text, omitted by mistake.

[[ ]] indicates that the letters or words within the brackets were crossed out by the writer.

Dots beneath letters indicate that the letters are not fully preserved on the tablet. In many cases we can be sure what the letters were either because enough survives to identify them or because the rest of the letters in the word make it obvious what the uncertain ones were. Subscript dots without any letters above them indicate surviving traces of letters which cannot be confidently identified. Subscript dots within square brackets indicate the number of letters calculated as missing.

In presenting the texts I have attempted to give a line-by-line translation into English, but it should be noted that the differences between Latin and English word order make it impossible to achieve an exact correspondence.

1 Account of food supplies

This is part of a daily record of food supplies used by the military unit at Vindolanda. The record itself has not survived completely and only a part of what has survived is given here. The whole account was in the form of a series of wooden leaves which were folded across the middle and tied to one another, thus forming a concertina type of wooden notebook (see above, fig. 11). This was obviously a convenient way of presenting accounts which generally are more appropriate to long, narrow columns than to broad, short ones such as are used in the letters.

Vegetius tells us that it was standard practice in the Roman army to keep careful records of all transactions of this kind. Accounts from Egypt show that army personnel were often sent out to requisition or purchase supplies for their units and it is very probable that the units in Britain acquired their food supplies from the surrounding area, though some special items like wine must have been imported. There were a number of officials in the unit responsible for the administration of what we would call the quartermaster's department and it seems likely that this account is a record kept by one such official for a period of several days in June of a year which is unfortunately not specified.

The account lists quantities of foodstuffs under consecutive date headings. This particular feature has one incidental bonus in that it enabled the various pieces of the account to be reassembled in the correct order. The quantities of food involved are fairly small and this suggests that the record is mainly concerned with disbursements of food from the quartermaster's store rather than acquisition. The word *allatus* in line 3, however, must refer to something 'brought in'. Part of the account (not given here) seems to concern payments of money as well, so this may be a notebook kept by one particular clerk recording a miscellany of transactions for which he was the official in charge.

The Roman soldier received basic rations of food, for which he had to pay. Army pay records show that the cost of food was deducted at source, along with various other items such as clothing. It is possible that some of the foodstuffs in this account were issued as part of basic rations but the text itself makes it clear that at least some of them were not. The phrases *per priuatum* ('through Privatus'—as the translation suggests, this might be a personal name or it might perhaps mean 'civilian'), *ad stipes* ('for charity') and *ad sacrum diuae* ('for the festival of the goddess') seem to indicate special transactions. All these phrases refer to the items which precede them, and one noticeable fact is that they only occur in the entries for 24 June which has a far larger number of items and a far greater variety of commodities than any other date heading. It is perhaps not a coincidence that this was the date of the Festival of *Fors Fortuna*, a deity particularly revered in the Roman army. A religious holiday might be a suitable occasion for making charitable donations or for individuals to obtain extra food supplies for a celebration.

The account itself, especially when considered in conjunction with the text which follows (no. 2), is interesting for the insight it gives us into the variety of foodstuffs in use in the army. One surprising fact is that *frumentum* (wheat), which was certainly a staple item in the military diet, is mentioned only once (in no. 2). *Hordeum* (barley) occurs frequently but it is generally believed that this was not much eaten by soldiers; its commonest use was as animal fodder and if Vindolanda was at this time garrisoned by a unit which included cavalry (a *cohors equitata*), the appearance of barley in the account could easily be explained. Alternatively, it might perhaps have been eaten by the soldiers at the end of the season when wheat was in short supply, or have been used in brewing or cooking (it was an ingredient of *polenta*, a sort of porridge).

The repeated occurrence of the word *cervesa* (it is more usually found in the form *cervesia* or *cervisia*) is also interesting. This was Celtic beer (the word itself is Celtic in origin) and it must have been common in Britain and Gaul. It is not hard to believe that the Roman soldiers in Britain (many of whom were recruited in the Gallic provinces) could have had a reputation for beer swilling! It was made, probably locally, by grain-malting and the cereal base could be either wheat or a grain called *bracis* (which appears in no. 2).

Vinum, which appears five times in this excerpt, was vintage wine, which was not normally part of soldiers' rations. One of the five references might indicate the import of an exceptionally high-class wine (see note 3), and another suggests that it was used in connection with the festival. Much more common amongst the ranks was the use of *acetum* (sour wine) which was normally mixed with water to make a drink called *posca*. Finally, there are references to fish-sauce (*muria*) and to *axungia* (pork-fat or lard) for which a wide variety of uses are known. Here it seems to have some connection with the charitable donations made on 24 June (see note 5).

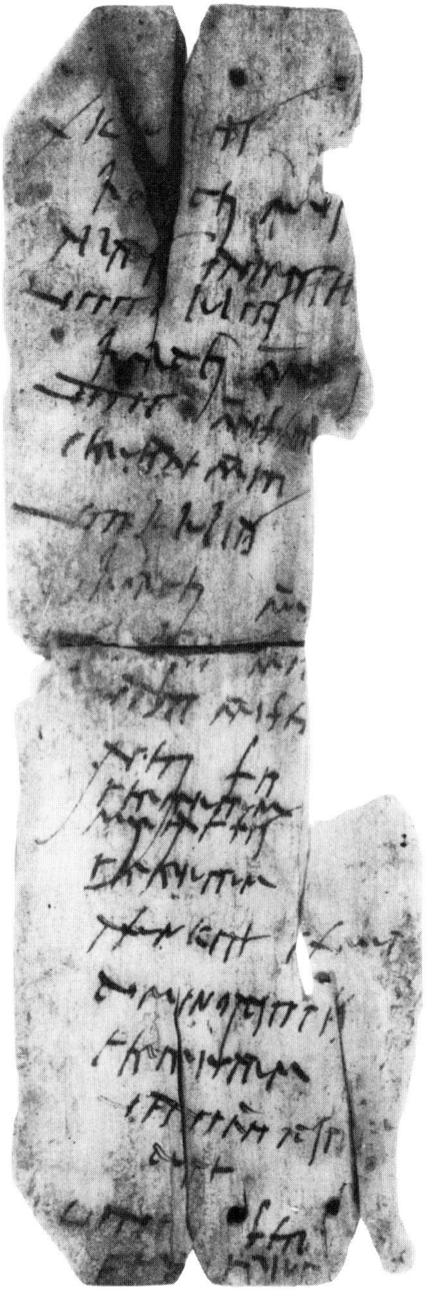

x K(alendas) Iulias[1]	22 June:
hordei m(odii)[2] v s(emis)	Of barley, 5 1/2 *modii.*
allatus ụini . . ssec[[3]	Of Massic wine (?), brought in . . .
viiii Ḳ(alendas) Iulias	23 June:
hordei m(odii) v s(emis)	Of barley, 5 1/2 *modii.*
uini m(odius) i (sextarii)[4] xiiii	Of wine, 1 *modius* 14 *sextarii.*
ceruesae m(odii) iii	Of Celtic beer, 3 *modii.*
viii K(alendas) Iulias	24 June:
hordei m(odii) vị . [	Of barley, 6+ *modii.*
c̣ẹṛụẹṣaẹ m(odii) iii (sextarii) . . .	Of Celtic beer, 3 *modii* . . . *sextarii.*
uini m(odius) i (sextarii) xii	Of wine, 1 *modius* 12 *sextarii.*
aceti (sextarii) ii	Of sour wine, 2 *sextarii,*
per priuatum	through Priuatus (?).
muriae (sextarii) i s(emis)	Of fish-sauce, 1 1/2 sextarii,
per p̣riuatum	through Priuatus (?).
axungiae (sextarii) xỵ	Of pork-fat, 15 *sextarii*
domino[5] ad stipes	to the lord for charitable donations,
per priuatum	through Priuatus (?).
uini m(odius) i ad sac̣ṛụṃ	Of wine, 1 *modius* for the festival
d<i>uae	of the goddess (?).
uini (sextarii) xii	Of wine, 12 *sextarii,*
per priuaṭụ[m	through Priuatus (?).

18 Tablet 1, scale 1:1.

1. This is the normal form in which Roman dates are expressed: ten days (counting inclusively) before the Kalends (first day) of July. *Kalendas* is written as a large K with no mark of abbreviation.

2. The measure in use here is the so-called *Italicus modius* which was approximately 8.6 litres. It was normally used as a measure for dry goods and it is a little surprising to find that this account also reckons liquids such as beer and wine in *modii*. The normal abbreviation is *m* with a flat dash above it, but this is sometimes omitted.

3. The word *allatus* means 'brought in' and must therefore refer to incoming supplies. The word after *vini* is difficult to read and explain. It might be *uini Massec[i]*; Massic wine, which came from Campania in Italy, had a particularly good reputation. If this is correct, it is interesting to find such a high-class product in northern Britain and one would guess that it was for the use of the officers only.

4. The symbol used for *sextarius* is *f*. There were sixteen *sextarii* to the *modius* and it is therefore a little over half a litre (see fig. 17).

5. It is impossible to be sure what the word *domino* ('to the lord') signifies. The word is not normally used to refer to a military commander, though it would be natural to suppose that he would be the appropriate person to make charitable donations (*stipes*), perhaps to the local civilian populace, on the occasion of a religious festival. The pork-fat, to which this phrase refers, might have been used in some kind of sacrifice or religious ceremony, or perhaps for making candles.

2 *Account of food supplies*

This account is similar to the preceding document in several respects but there are also some important and interesting differences. The surviving part consists of a single leaf of wood which has been folded across the middle. As in the other account, the writing is parallel with the short edge of the leaf, thus giving us a long, narrow column. Unfortunately since the top and the bottom of the leaf have been lost, we cannot be sure whether it will have had tie-holes which were used to attach it to the preceding or following leaf. But it is possible that the whole text was written on this single, folded leaf and that there was a date heading in the part lost at the top and some kind of a final total at the bottom.

This is not part of the same series of accounts as the previous document. For one thing, the hands are distinctly different; this account is the work of a writer who uses tall, slim letter forms with a distinct tendency to slope to the right. Although both accounts deal with foodstuffs, it is remarkable that there is no item in the one which recurs in the other. It is probable that most of the items in no. 1 were disbursed from the quartermaster's store at Vindolanda, but no. 2 is much easier to explain by the supposition that it records purchases made on behalf of the military unit at Vindolanda.

The account lists four different kinds of meat and four non-meat items. The loss of the right-hand side of the document means that most of the entries are not complete, but it is noticeable that in the case of the two non-meat items where the word is complete the genitive case is used (*salis*, 'of salt'; *bracis*, 'of emmer'). It is probable that these will have been followed by a measure (*modii* or *sextarii*) and a quantity as in no. 1. Genitive endings have been supplied for the other two non-meat items (*condimenta*, 'spices' and *frumentum*, 'wheat') by analogy. The meats, however, are all in the accusative (direct object) case but, unfortunately, in the only case where there is any trace of writing after the name of the meat (*pernam*, 'ham') it is not possible to read it with any confidence. However, there exists a very similar account from the Roman province of Dacia (now part of Rumania) which has an entry in the form *porcellum* (*denarii*) *v* (which can be translated as 'young pig at a price of five *denarii*'). It seems reasonable to suppose that this was the form of the meat entries in the Vindolanda text.

The most notable feature of no. 2 is the high proportion of meat and its variety. This rather contradicts the common belief that Roman soldiers ate very little meat and then only on special occasions such as festivals. But recent archaeological studies of bone remains in Roman forts have shown that, in fact, a good deal of meat was consumed and the animal remains at Vindolanda certainly fit this picture. So it is interesting that this account tends to confirm the archaeological picture and all the meats mentioned (except perhaps venison) were reasonably common. It is impossible to be sure, however, that this list represents the soldier's regular diet, as opposed to officers' rations or special commodities for a feast. But there is a strong presumption, on the basis of the entry in line 12 (see note 5), that at least some of the items were for daily use.

19 Tablet 2, scale 1:1.

	]in p̣[[1]	. . . in . . .
	]ṣ (denarii)[2] [	. . . *denarii* . . .
	condimen[torum	Of spices . . .
	capream[3] [	Roe-deer . . .
	salis[4] . [	Of salt . . .
	porcellum [	Young pig . . .
	pernam . [	Ham . . .
	in p̣[	In . . .
	frumen[ti	Of wheat . . .
	ceruin[am	Venison . . .
	in p . [	In . . .
	ad cotidiạ[n[5]	For daily . . .
	caprea[m	Roe-deer . . .
2nd hand?	[[s(umma) (denarii)[6] [	
1st hand?	s(umma) (denarii) xx [	Total *denarii* 20 . . .
	braciṣ[7] [	Of emmer . . .
	(denarii) ị[	*Denarii* 1 +
	] . ụm[[8]	Total (?) . . .
	Text breaks off (?)	

1. Some of this line is lost and the content can only be guessed at. It might have been, for example, *in praetorio*, referring to the headquarters of the commanding officer at the fort. This would, of course, carry the implication that most of these supplies were destined for the top brass, especially since the same phrase probably recurs in lines 8 and 11.

2. The account uses the normal symbol for the *denarius*, ✕.

3. *Caprea* (the only meat item which occurs more than once) is the Latin name for the roe-deer which certainly existed in the vicinity of Vindolanda in Roman times. In the Middle Ages and later its meat was regarded as inferior to that of red and fallow deer. Fallow deer were not introduced into this area until the thirteenth century so it seems likely that the reference to *cervina* in line 10, which is best translated as 'venison', applies to the meat of the red deer.

4. The salt might have been intended as a preservative for the meat.

5. The implication here is that at least the entry immediately following (roe-deer) was intended for daily use.

6. The line was crossed through several times by the writer, presumably because he made a mistake in his calculation. In fact, the following line, giving the 'correct' total, may be the work of another writer, in which case he was also probably responsible for the deletion.

7. This is a Gallic name for a kind of cereal which could be used for malting. It is known to have been a basis for making Celtic beer (*cervesa*) which is mentioned in no. 1. It is interesting that the word found its way into modern Spanish in the form *cerveza*.

8. It is possible that the word *summa* was written out in full here, as indicating the final total for the whole account.

3 *Letter of recommendation*

Flavius Cerialis, to whom this letter is addressed, was the commander (*praefectus*) of the Eighth Cohort of Batavians, one of the auxiliary units which garrisoned Vindolanda in the period between about AD 95 and 105. Although the unit itself will have been recruited in an area which is now part of the Netherlands, Cerialis himself will probably have been of Italian or southern Gallic origin. Commissioned officers in the Roman army were of high status—belonging to either the senatorial or equestrian order—and came from the most 'Romanised' part of the Empire. Auxiliary units (as opposed to legions) were commanded by officers of equestrian status who would hold their commission for a period of two or three years before moving on.

The collection contains several letters addressed to Cerialis and, as one might expect, they seem to have come from a variety of people. Most of them are not otherwise known, but the identity of this correspondent is particularly intriguing. The surname Karus is preserved but, unfortunately, only the end of his 'family name' (*gentilicium*) survives. But it is possible that the writer might be identical with a man named Caius Julius Karus whose career is known from an inscription found in Africa. This man came from the province of Gallia Narbonensis (modern Provence), was commander of a Spanish unit, the Second Cohort of Asturians, and received military decorations whilst commanding this unit in a 'war' fought in Britain. The 'war' probably occurred during the period between about AD 90 and 110. The whole tone of the letter suggests that the writer and addressee are of roughly equivalent rank and status, as would be the case if they were both prefects of auxiliary units. Unfortunately, there is no clue as to the station of the Asturian cohort, but it is quite likely that it was in the northern frontier region and that Karus's 'war' was some military action connected with the Roman withdrawal from southern Scotland, which was taking place in the first decade of the second century.

The content of the letter is also of considerable interest. It is a letter of recommendation, intended to secure support and help from Cerialis. Examples of this genre are well known in letters written by literary men like Cicero and Pliny the Younger, who frequently wrote to influential friends on behalf of younger or less elevated acquaintances. The Vindolanda letter is, however, rather to be compared with the very few examples known from the papyri and it shows the importance of such patronage at a rather lower social level. It reinforces powerfully the general impression that such support was vital, particularly in army circles, for those who wished to gain promotion or a more favourable posting. The general prevalence of the practice is shown, at just about this same time, by an Egyptian recruit in Alexandria who complained in a letter to his father that 'here nothing is achieved without money and letters of recommendation are of no value unless one has assisted oneself.'

The examples of letters of recommendation in literature and on papyrus show the use of various common expressions or phrases which are appropriate to the genre and the Vindolanda letter fits the pattern very well. It is slightly unusual in that Cerialis is asked, in effect, not only to support the person being recommended but also to pass on his recommendation to another person. The identity of these people is also of interest. The person recommended is called Brigionus, and this is clearly a Romanised form of a Celtic name which is probably Gallic in origin. We cannot tell whether he was actually a soldier himself; but he will certainly have been a person of fairly modest social standing who was evidently attempting to use connections with Roman officers to advance himself.

The person to whom the recommendation is to be passed on is called Annius Equester, a centurion 'in charge of the region' (*regionarius*), at Luguvalium (Carlisle). This is by far the earliest example of the use of this title, and it is very interesting to find such a command attested at Carlisle during a period when its military importance will have been great. The 'region' is presumably a geographical area which might include a number of communities or settlements. The centurion himself, who will have had a number of legionary soldiers under his command, was probably detached from the famous Ninth Legion which was stationed at York until at least AD 107–8. Perhaps he was put in charge of operations in part of the western sector of the Stanegate frontier during the period when the Romans were completing the withdrawal from southern Scotland.

It is worth noting, finally, that Karus did not actually write the main part of the letter himself. He was probably responsible for adding the final greeting (*vale, frater*) which is in a hand different from that of the rest of the text, presumably that of a clerk or scribe. The practice was very common—we might recall, for instance, that St Paul emphasised at the end of the Epistle to the Colossians that the greeting was in his own hand.

20 *Tablet 3, scale 1:1½.*

i

[. . .]ịus Karuṣ C̣[e]ṛ[iali
su]ọ ṣ[alutem.
. . . .] Brigionus petiṭ[1] a ṃẹ
[domi]ne ut eum tibi coṃ-
ṃẹṇdareṭ.[2] rogo ergo do-
ṃịṇẹ ṣị quod[3] a te petieriṭ
[ut u]ẹḷịṣ ẹi subscribere.
Annịọ Ẹquesṭri (c̣ẹṇṭuṛịọṇị)[4] ṛegi-
onarịo Luguualio[5] ro-
go ut eum commen-

ii

[. . . .] ḍigneriṣ . [. . . .
. . .] . que nom[ine
ḍebetorem[6] m[e tibi
obligaturus. ọp[to
te felicissiṃ[um
bene ụạḷẹṛẹ.[7]
blank

2nd hand uale, frater.

Back C]ẹṛịali
praẹf̣(ecto)[8]

. . . ius Karus to his Cerialis,
greeting.
. . . Brigionus has requested me,
my lord, to recommend him
to you. I therefore ask,
my lord, that if he has made any request of you,
you consent to give him your approval.
I ask that you think fit to
recommend him to Annius Equester, centurion
in charge of the region,

at Luguvalium,
by doing which you will place me
in debt to you both in his
name and my own. I hope that
you are enjoying the best of fortune
and are in good health.

2nd hand Farewell, brother.

Back To Cerialis,
prefect.

1. The name *Brigio* occurs on an inscription from Germany (Mainz). Here it looks as if it has simply acquired a Latin termination. The word '*petit.*' is a contracted form of the perfect tense, *petivit* or *petiit*. This letter, like many of the Vindolanda texts, shows grammatical and phonological usages which do not conform to the rules and practices of classical literary Latin. But such phenomena provide valuable evidence for the way in which Latin was spoken and written at lower social levels. For more examples see the following notes.

2. The writer intended, and should have written, the first person singular *commendarem* here. It is possible that he clumsily corrected the final *t* to *m*.

3. According to the 'rules' of the grammar book one would expect to find *quid* here.

4. The symbol for *centurioni* is a sickle-shaped sign, ʒ.

5. Luguvalium is Carlisle. The derivation is from the personal name LUGUUALOS, 'he whose strength is like (the god) Lugus' or 'strong in (the god) Lugus'.

6. *Debitorem* would be the 'normal' form but the interchange of *i* and *e* is very common in vulgar Latin.

7. This is a very common type of closing formula and such expressions are almost universal in personal letters of this kind.

8. The address is written, as is normal in the Vindolanda letters, on the back of the right-hand section of the leaf. The military unit is not named, but one other letter does include it in the address.

4 *Draft of a letter*

This tablet contains the greater part of twenty-six lines of a letter and it is remarkable in that, unlike the other letters in the collection, it is written on *both* sides of a single leaf of wood. It is also unusual in that it lacks the name of the sender of the letter. In three places a word or words are crossed out. These unusual features indicate that what we have is only a draft and it is probable that the writer, having made the rough copy, would then pass it on to a clerk to add the name of the sender and the final greeting and make a fair copy. The sender himself might then have added a final valediction in his own hand (as in no. 3). If there were any doubt about the nature of this text, it is completely dispelled by the fact that the writer actually states at the end of the letter *haec tibi a Vindolanda scribo* ('I am writing this to you from Vindolanda'). There could hardly be a more evocative phrase to enable us to bridge the gulf of almost two thousand years between the writer and the present-day reader.

This letter is important for a number of reasons. First and foremost is the fact that it mentions a certain Marcellus and identifies him as the governor of Britain. In spite of the fact that the full name has not survived there can be no doubt that this is Lucius Neratius Marcellus, who is known from the evidence of a military diploma to have been holding this office in AD 103. This is worth stressing because it is the only piece of information in the content of the writing tablets which allows us to corroborate the date for the collection deduced from the archaeological context (*c.* AD 95–105). This Marcellus is also known from a letter of Pliny the Younger, who used his acquaintance with Marcellus to obtain from him, when he was governor of Britain, the grant of a military commission for Suetonius, the biographer of the Roman Emperors.

The writer does not give his name and we cannot say who he was. But the letter is exceptional for the quality of the Latin which has a literary flavour and some pretensions to elegance. It can therefore be said with confidence that the writer belonged to the officer class. The tablet is also very interesting for the style of the handwriting. It joins letters boldly and more frequently than other hands; it uses many of the ordinary cursive forms of letters in a rather idiosyncratic way; and it often leaves a space between words.

It is not easy to reconstruct the text in its entirety, partly because it is impossible to be sure how much, if anything, is lost at the foot of the tablet. The text printed below omits two lines on the front (at the foot) and one line at the very end because these are too fragmentary to offer any sense. But the general point seems clear. The addressee, Crispinus, is in a position to exercise influence with the governor, perhaps having recently obtained a post on his staff. The writer is asking Crispinus to use his influence on his (the writer's) behalf to make his military service pleasant by putting him on good terms with as many influential people as possible.

It should be noted that the translation aims at reproducing a general sense which is sometimes dependent on hypothetical reconstructions of missing parts of the Latin text. These cannot be set out in detail here, but a full discussion may be found in the monograph by A. K. Bowman and J. D. Thomas (cited on p. 48, below).

*21 Tablet 4 (*front*), lines 1–12 (the last two lines are omitted from the transcription). Scale 1:1.*

Front

[ ] *blank* Crispino[1] suo [*blank* ?
G]ṛattịo Crispino redeunte . [. . .
. . . .] ⟦non fui mihi⟧ et . ḍ . [. .
. . . . li]benter amplexụṣ ṣ[um do-
ṃine ṣạlutandi te ọc̣c̣ạṣṣịọṇẹṃ[2]
[d]ọminum meum et quem saluom
⟦ḥạbere⟧ esse et omnis spei
⟦suạe⟧ compotem inter praecipuạ
uoti habeo. hoc enim de
me semper meruisti usque
ad hanc ḍ[ignit]ạtem.[3] cuius fịḍ-[4]

To his Crispinus.
Since Grattius Crispinus is returning to . . .
and . . .
I have gladly seized the opportunity, my
lord, of greeting you,
you who are my lord and the man whom
I most especially wish to be
in good health and master of
all your hopes. For you have always
deserved this of me right up to
this present high office. . . .

22 *Tablet 4 (back), lines 14–25 (the last line is omitted from the transcription). Scale 1:1.*

Back

[. . . . .]m Marcẹllum[5] clarissị[mum ui-
rum] consularem meum. quar . [. . . .
oc]c̣assionem nunc ut . [. . . . .
. . .] ṭibi amicorum dọ[. . . . .
sụạ [p]ṛạẹsentia.[6] quos tụ[. . . . .
illius scio plurimos haberẹ [. . . .
quomodo uoụes imple quidq[uid
de te exspecto et me . ḷụ . [.] . . .
aṃicis ita instrue ut beneficio
tuo militiam [po]ṣṣim iucundam
experiri. ha[ec ti]bi a Uindolan-
ḍa[7]scribo . [. . . . . .] hiberna [

Lucius Marcellus, that most distinguished man,
my governor. He therefore offers (?)
you the opportunity now of
. . . the talents of your friends
through his presence. Of those whom you protect with
his permission, very many, I know, get what they want
just as you promise. Fulfil what
I expect of you and . . .
so furnish me with friends that thanks to you
I may be able to enjoy a term of military service
which is pleasant. I am writing this to you from
Vindolanda where my winter-quarters are (?) . . .

1. A man named Crispinus is known from other letters to have commanded the First Cohort of Tungrians which was at Vindolanda during this period, probably succeeding the Eighth Batavian Cohort as the garrison force. But it is not likely that either the addressee or the Grattius Crispinus mentioned in the next line is this commander. The name Crispinus is a very common one.

2. The whole phrase '*libenter . . . occassionem*' has a very elegant and literary flavour. The normal form of the last word is *occasio*, but the reduplication of *s* is common in vulgar Latin.

3. In this context the word *dignitatem* would mean a high office held by the addressee.

4. The next two lines are too fragmentary to reproduce here. The word following *cuius* was probably *fiducia* ('confidence'), indicating the writer's reliance on his relationship with the addressee.

5. There does not seem to be room for the name Lucius Neratius Marcellus to be written in full; but it was quite common, especially for upper-class Romans, to be referred to simply by the forename and surname, omitting the family name. So it is probable that the text simply had *Lucium Marcellum*.

6. This section is very difficult to reconstruct; '*do*[' is perhaps to be understood as the beginning of the word *dotes* ('talents'), with which one might supply a verb with the sense of 'helping along'.

7. This is important because it confirms the spelling used in antiquity. The literary sources which name the place all have slightly garbled versions of the name. But the correct form has been deduced from an inscription which refers to the townspeople of Vindolanda as *vicani Vindolandesses* (*-ss-* here is not a reduplication, but represents *-ns-*).

5 *Letter about clothing*

This tablet has the distinction of being the first to be recognised as such in the excavation season of 1973. It is unfortunately incomplete and contains only parts of two columns of a letter written on a folded leaf of wood. It is certain that a fair proportion of the tops of the columns is missing and something may be lost at the end. The text presents us with the closing greeting of the main body of the letter but it is possible that the sender may have added a valedictory phrase (as in no. 3).

The letter was evidently sent to a soldier serving at Vindolanda. The writer mentions various items of clothing and it seems probable that he or she is a solicitous relative or friend whose concern for the recipient's material comfort led him or her to send 'a parcel from home'. There are several letters on papyrus from Egypt which refer to this custom, in particular one in which a recruit serving in the Alexandrian fleet wrote home to ask his family to send him some items of clothing. This suggests that our Vindolanda letter takes us away from the world of the Roman officer and into that of the ordinary ranker and there are some other signs of this in our text. The names listed in the second half of the letter do not look like those of officers and the word *contibernales* (*sic*) also suggests the world of the ordinary soldier; these are members of the *contubernium*, the soldier's mess. This would then be one of the few examples of letters emanating from a somewhat humbler social stratum and it is interesting to reflect on the degree of literacy which this indicates.

The items of clothing mentioned are of some interest. *Udones* are socks made of wool or felt. The two references to pairs of sandals (*solearum*, see fig. 6) might remind us of a relief from Wroxeter showing a British legionary soldier wearing sandals, or the Roman soldiers on Trajan's Column (fig. 18). *Subligaria* are Roman underpants. Pliny the Elder says that they were worn by workmen in the frankincense factories in Alexandria, meaning, presumably, that they were the only garment worn!

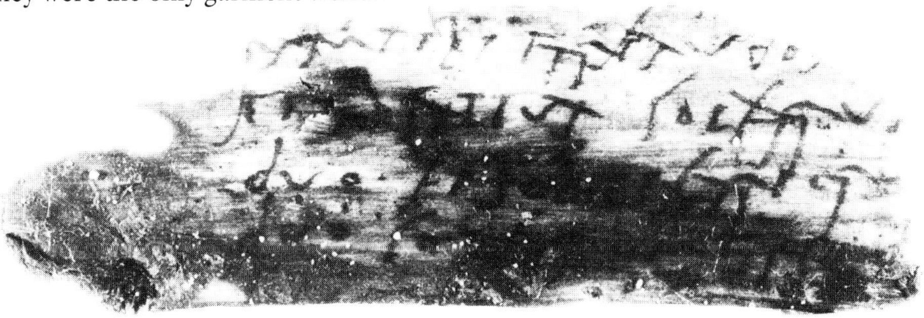

23 Tablet 5, fragment i. Scale 1:1.

traces	
ṛam[1] tibi paria udọ[num	. . . I have sent (?) you . . . pairs of socks
ṭ . ab Sattua[2] solearuṃ [	from Sattua two pairs of sandals
duo et subligarioruṃ [	and two pairs of underpants,
duo solearum paria dụ[o	two pairs of sandals . . .
traces	

24 Tablet 5, fragment ii. Scale 1:1.

]um ṣaluṭaṛẹ . [
]ṇdem Elpidem[3]Ịụ[
] . enum Tetrịcum et omṇ[es
c]ontibernales[4] cum quibus [
o]pto felicissimus uiuas.[5] (*blank*) [
traces

Greet . . .
. . ndes, Elpis, Iu . . .,
. . . enus, Tetricus and all
your messmates with whom
I hope that you live in the greatest good fortune

1. The line must begin with the last part of a verb. The most likely restoration is *miseram* ('I had sent').

2. Sattua is most probably a personal name, Celtic in origin.

3. '*Elpidem*' is a curiosity. It is a Greek name which the Romans used in the form Elpis or Helpis, sometimes Latinising it as Elpidius or Helpidius. In Greek the name is normally, but not always, feminine. The Romans used it as a masculine name and it is likely to be so here if it refers to someone serving in a military unit (though the archaeological finds at Vindolanda clearly indicate the presence of camp-followers of both sexes). Perhaps the most surprising thing is to find a Greek-derived name in north Britain at such an early date.

4. The normal form is *contubernales* but the spelling with *i* is common in inscriptions. It means quite literally the members of the recipient's mess.

5. The closing greeting is unusual in its use of the verb *vivere* ('to live'); *valere* ('to be in good health') is much more common in formulae of this sort.

6 *Private letter*

This incomplete letter is addressed to a *decurio* (officer of a cavalry squadron) named Lucius. The hand in which it is written is a neat and regular one, with well-formed letters made with thick strokes, and the writer has attempted, at least in some places, to leave small spaces between the words. The main point of interest in the letter is the fact that the writer refers to a gift of fifty oysters which came from a place called Cordonovi, unfortunately not identifiable. Remains of oyster-shells have been found at many archaeological sites in Britain, so oysters were perhaps not quite as expensive a delicacy as they are today.

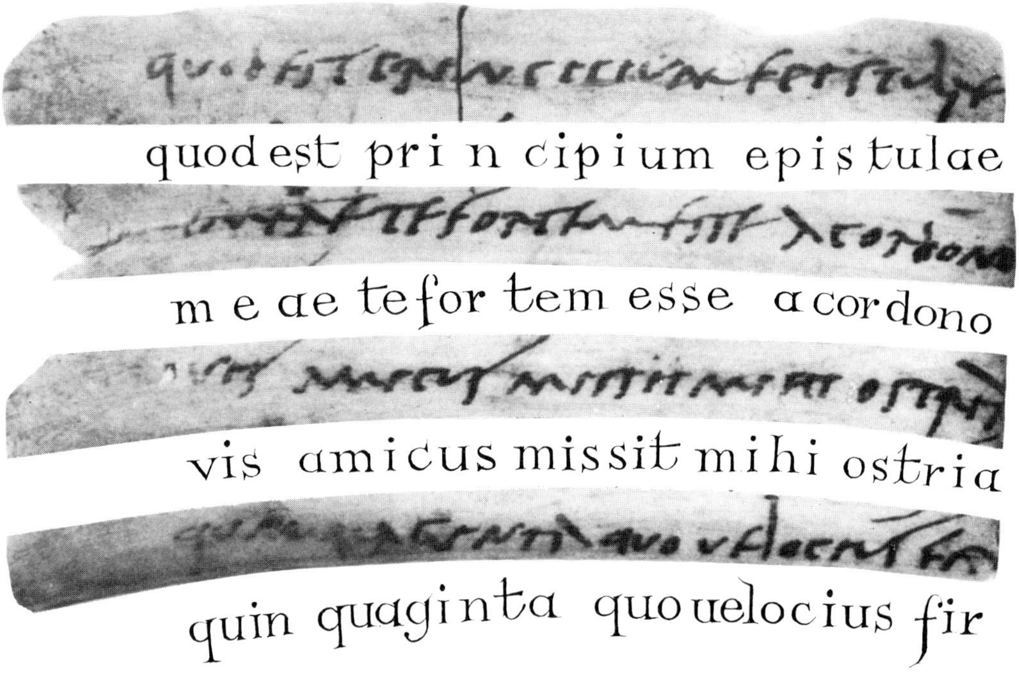

25 Tablet 6. Scale 1:1 2/3.

quod est principium epistulae
meae te fortem esse. a Cordono-
uis amicus missit mihi ostria
quinquaginta. quo uelocius fiṛ

Back Lucio decurion[i]

. . . which is the first point of my letter (to hope ?)
that you are vigorous. From Cordonovi
a friend has sent me fifty
oysters. In order that . . . more speedily . . .

Back To Lucius, decurion

Further reading

All of the Vindolanda writing tablets are published with detailed commentaries by A. K. Bowman and J. D. Thomas in *Vindolanda: the Latin Writing Tablets* (*Britannia*, Monograph no. 4, 1983). The texts presented in this pamphlet are there published as nos 4, 5, 22, 37, 38 and 39.

For a fuller description of the general importance of Vindolanda see R. E. Birley, *Vindolanda, a Roman Frontier Post on Hadrian's Wall* (Thames & Hudson, 1977). On Hadrian's Wall see D. J. Breeze and B. Dobson, *Hadrian's Wall* (Allen Lane, 1976).

On Roman Britain in general: S. S. Frere, *Britannia, a History of Roman Britain* (3rd edn, Routledge & Kegan Paul, 1978); P. Salway, *Roman Britain* (Oxford University Press, 1981); J. S. Wacher, *Roman Britain* (Dent, 1980); A. R. Birley, *The People of Roman Britain* (Batsford, 1979); T. W. Potter, *Roman Britain* (British Museum Publications, 1983).

On the army in Britain: P. A. Holder, *The Army of Roman Britain* (Batsford, 1983).

A good description of most aspects of life in the Roman army is given by G. R. Watson in *The Roman Soldier* (Thames & Hudson, 1969); see also G. Webster, *The Roman Imperial Army of the First and Second Centuries A.D.* (2nd edn, Methuen, 1979). The fullest collection of documentary evidence for the Roman army is R. O. Fink, *Roman Military Records on Papyrus* (*Philological Monographs of the American Philological Association*, no. 26, 1971).